# I Want A Kitten Or A Cat
# Best Pets for Kids - Book 3

## Tristan Pulsifer and
## Jacquelyn Elnor Johnson

www.CrimsonHillBooks.com/best-pets-for-kids

First edition, June 2017.

**Cataloguing in Publication Data**

Pulsifer, Tristan | Johnson, Jacquelyn Elnor

I Want A Kitten or a Cat | Best Pets For Kids Series

Description: Crimson Hill Books trade paperback edition | Nova Scotia, Canada

ISBN 978-1-988650-21-0 (Paperback)

BISAC: JNF003040 Juvenile Nonfiction: Animals - Cats | JNF003170 Juvenile Nonfiction: Animals - Pets | JNF051150 Juvenile Nonfiction: Science & Nature - Zoology

THEMA: WNGC - Cats as pets | YNNH2 - Children's / Teenage general interest: Pets & pet care: cats | YNNJ22 - Children's / Teenage general interest: Cats

Record available at https://www.bac-lac.gc.ca/eng/Pages/home.aspx

Cover Image: AlexasFotos via Pixabay
Cover design: Jacquelyn Elnor Johnson
Book design and formatting: Jesse Johnson

Crimson Hill Books
(a division of)
Crimson Hill Products Inc.
Wolfville, Nova Scotia
Canada

# Contents

# Chapter One

# What's It Like To Have A Pet Kitten Or A Cat?

*This ginger kitten is almost six months old.*

What is the most popular pet in the world?

The answer is "cats." There are more than 600 million pet cats in the world. That's about three times as many as the second most popular pet; dogs.

This book tells you all about kittens and cats – what it's like to have a kitten or cat, where to find your new pet, what he or she needs to be healthy and happy, how to deal with 'bad' cat behaviour and ideas for what to name your cat.

## What makes cats so popular as pets?

Maybe it's because they're so cute. All cats have big eyes. Their eyes are the biggest of any animal, when compared to their face size and body size.

Having big eyes is one of the things that really appeals to humans. We think that creatures with big eyes, short noses and small chins are adorable. The reason for this is that big eyes, short noses and small chins remind us of human babies' faces.

It isn't just that we like faces that look like this. Our bodies release a hormone that makes us like them and want to protect them. Hormones are chemicals in our bodies that control growing and can cause us to behave in certain ways.

Because of one hormone, babies and small animals with big eyes have a power over us! They can make us want to protect them and love them.

Some of the special things about having a pet cat are they can be good companions.

They like being with people.

They are easy to care for.

They are soft and furry.

Their purring is very soothing to people. Stress is a known cause of many illnesses, some of them serious. This means cats can help keep their owners healthy!

Most cats aren't interested in car rides and usually aren't good travellers. They prefer the comforts of home.

But, like people and all pets, they need proper food, a warm and safe home and, occasionally, good medical care.

Also like people, they sometimes act badly. Or make mistakes. They might scratch your furniture, or throw up on the rug, or meow loudly when you want to go to sleep. In this book, we will talk about all these 'bad cat' things and how to teach your cat better manners.

Here are some other things you need to be prepared for about cats. They shed hair and need to have their coats brushed.

If you let them outside, they like to hunt. They will kill mice and songbirds. You might not care about the mice, but cats killing songbirds is a serious problem. Some of the birds we enjoy seeing in our gardens are close to being endangered and could become extinct in this century (extinct means they die out completely). The answer is to keep your cat indoors, or else put bells on her or his collar to warn the birds to stay away from a hunting cat.

## Who wouldn't like having a cat?

If you already have a senior dog or elderly cat, it isn't fair to expect them to put up with a bouncy kitten.

*This terrier doesn't look like he's quite ready to be a kitten babysitter.*

If you are away from home almost all the time, it isn't fair to pets to be left alone too much.

And if you are planning to move, or renovating your home (renovating means making a lot of changes like building a new garage) now probably isn't the time to adopt a new pet.

## What cats like

Cats are homebodies. They like there to be lots of comfy, warm places to take a nap.

They enjoy looking outside at birds, drinking water out of your glass, being up high on a top shelf so they can look down at their world, sitting on laps, eating fish, cozy hiding places, toys to play with and catnip.

They like it when you scratch them behind the ears, but don't like it when you pat their head.

Just like kids, cats have individual personalities. Some are more curious than others. Some are more talky than others. Some are friendlier than others. Some are more fussy than others. Part of the fun of adopting a kitten or a cat is getting to know who they really are.

I Want A Kitten Or A Cat

# Chapter Two

# All About Kittens

*This Bengal queen is content to be feeding her kittens.*

A mother cat is called a Queen. Queens are pregnant for about 63 days, or just a bit longer than eight weeks. Then they give birth to two, three, four, or as many as seven kittens. The most kittens a queen ever had at one time was 18!

It is very unusual for a queen to have more than seven kittens. But a healthy queen can have babies three or four times a year. This means a mother cat, or queen, could have more than 30 babies in one year! Over the course of her lifetime, she could have hundreds of babies!

*Be careful how you pick up a kitten or a cat. Always put one hand firmly under them first and your other hand on top, to keep them from slipping and falling. Never pick them up by grabbing one leg, their tail, or the skin at the back of their neck.*

At first, the kittens are so tiny you could easily hold one in your hand. Each kitten weighs only about 3

ounces (or 85 grams). That's about the same as a small apple weighs. Or half as much as an average orange weighs!

Kittens are blind and deaf for their first week of life. They can't see or hear anything. They need their mother's help to start breathing and find their way to her nipples to get cat milk.

New kittens sleep almost all the time when they aren't drinking their mother's milk. They sleep so much because they need all their strength to grow quickly.

*This little guy is just one month old. He's too little to leave his mother and litter-mates yet.*

When they are about one week old, they open their eyes for the first time.

All kittens have blue eyes at first. Most kittens' eyes change colour to yellow, orange, copper or green before they are adults.

When kittens are four, five or six weeks old, they learn how to walk. Soon they are bouncing around, pouncing on each other and always exploring. They can get into plenty of trouble!

They do lots of play fighting with their brothers and sisters. This is how they start to learn pouncing and hunting skills.

Their mother, the queen, will push them away when it is time for them to learn how to eat and drink from

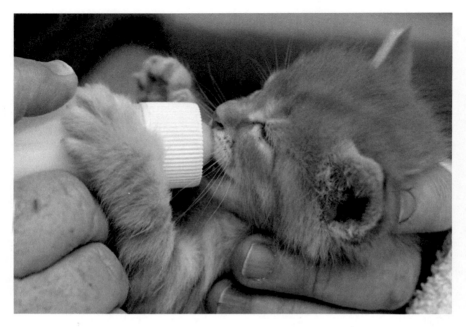

*This tiny rescue kitten lost her mother. She needs to be bottle-fed cat formula until she is old enough to eat regular cat food.*

their food dishes, if they are indoor cats. She will show them how to do this. She will also show them where the litter box is and how to use it.

If the queen and her kittens are outdoor cats or feral cats, the queen will teach her kittens how to avoid danger, find safe shelter and hunt for food. Feral means they live in a barn or outdoors. They are wild.

A feral queen will also protect her kittens from harm until they are big enough to protect themselves.

All female cats are good mothers. They teach their kittens everything they need to know about how to stay healthy, warm and safe.

All kittens need to be touched and held by people to grow up to be good pets. They must have a chance to get used to people and learn to trust that people will be kind to them.

Feral cats are usually afraid of people. They don't know how to live as pets.

But a feral baby kitten can be raised to be a good pet. This is only true if that kitten has been handled and cared for by a gentle and kind person and taught how to get along with people. This must happen before the kitten is 7 weeks old. After that, it's usually much harder for a feral kitten to learn how to be an indoor pet cat.

Kittens have very tiny claws that are as sharp as needles! If your cat has kittens, you will want to wear clothing that covers your arms and legs any time you are near the kittens. This is because kittens will climb up anything, including you!

If you aren't careful, their sharp little claws will scratch you.

Kittens are old enough to leave their mother when they can find their own food and no longer need her milk to survive. The longer kittens can stay with the queen, the more they learn about being good pets.

Kittens need to be about four months old to be old enough to leave their mother and litter-mates (this means their brothers and sisters) and adjust to their new home.

Some breeds of cats are old enough to leave their mother a bit sooner than age 4 months.

Kittens grow into adult cats when they are between six months and one year old. By then, their eyes and possibly their fur has changed colour. They are old enough to become parents and have their own kittens.

# Chapter Three

# All About Cats

Cats and people have lived together for a very long time. At least 10,000 years, scientists tell us.

So it isn't surprising that people have made up stories about cats. There are lots of stories, like Felix the Cat and Garfield, Heathcliff and Dinah in **Alice in Wonderland**.

There are also stories people tell about cats that aren't true. Cats can not see in the dark. They are very good at surviving, but they do not have nine lives. And they do not try to hurt babies or little children.

Another thing a lot of people believe about cats, but it's not true, is that all cats really like to drink milk. Most cats are allergic to cow or goat milk. Many people are also allergic to cow or goat milk.

Cats are meat eaters. This means they only eat birds, meat, fish or poultry. Poultry means chicken, turkey, geese or ducks.

Millions of years ago, when the earliest cats first appeared, they were able to eat a much larger variety of foods, including vegetables, grains and grasses.

No one knows exactly why cats lost this ability. Modern cats can eat some fruits, in very small amounts. They can't eat vegetables, seeds, nuts or grains.

*This female liger lives at the Big Cat Rescue Center in Florida.*

## What do pet cats eat?

Some owners make their cat food. But most prefer to buy cat food that is already made at the grocery store. It can be dry food (it comes in paper bags) or wet cat food (it comes in cans or plastic containers).

This food is specially made to have the right nutrition for cats. They can't eat dog food, which doesn't have some of the things in it cats need to stay healthy.

## How big do cats get?

The largest cat in the world is the liger, a creature

that is half tiger and half lion. Usually, a liger's father is a lion and their mother is a tiger.

An adult male liger can be more than 900 pounds (408 kg) and almost 11 feet (3.35 meters) long. But this big animal does not live in the wild, where lions and tigers do not ever have babies together. The world's only ligers live in zoos or animal conservation parks. They are very gentle animals.

The largest wild cat is the Siberian tiger. They live in Russia, China and North Korea, but they are endangered. There are only about 500 Siberian tigers left in the world.

The largest pet cat breeds are Maine Coon and Ragdoll cats. They can get to be about twice as big as other breeds of pet cats.

## How small can cats be?

The smallest breed of pet cats is the rusty-spotted cat. Another small breed is the singapura (say it like this: SING-ga-pure-a). They are usually less than half as big as tabby cats.

## How long do cats live?

Sadly, feral cats have short lives. There are many dangers in the world for wild cats. Sometimes, they cannot find enough food. Feral cats usually only live to be a few years old.

Pet cats can live much longer. The average lifetime for an outdoor cat is about 11 to 13 years. This is because of the dangers outside for cats, such as

*This is a Ragdoll kitten.*

fighting with other cats or dogs, outside poisons such as garden weed-killer or eating bugs or insects that carry illnesses. But the biggest danger for outdoor cats is being hit by a car.

Indoor cats miss all the excitement of exploring and hunting outside. But, because they are protected, they can live for much longer. With good food and good care, indoor cats almost always live past their 15th birthday. It isn't unusual to hear of a cat that is in his 20s. And a few cats live until they are 30, or more!

## How do cats drink?

Cats lap up their water. They aren't using their tongue like a spoon. Instead, they get water on the bottom side of their tongue and then into their mouths.

If you've ever tried to lean over and lap up water or milk from a bowl that is on the floor, you know it is just about impossible for a human to do! But cats and dogs, and some other animals, do it naturally.

## Why do cats purr?

Some cats purr; some roar. The wild cats that roar, such as lions, tigers and jaguars, don't know how to purr. Pet cats don't know how to roar.

It seems that some cats first learned how to purr when they moved in with people. But why did they do this? Some scientists say because the people liked it. To get along with people, the cats just kept purring.

But it could just be that a cat feels good when he or she is purring. When cats purr, their vocal cords (skin and muscles in the throat that make sound possible)

*Sleepy kitten.*

vibrate. Vibrate means move back and forth very quickly.

Cats purr both while breathing in and breathing out.

They purr at about the same speed as a diesel engine when it is idling (this means the engine is turned on, but the car or truck isn't moving). This sound is a steady "hummm" that is soothing to humans.

Tiny kittens purr to let their mother know they are getting enough milk. Cats also purr gently when they are sitting on your lap and being petted or having their fur gently brushed.

Gentle, soft purring means a happy cat.

But loud purring means a cat is in pain. If your cat is suddenly purring very loudly, they need to go to the vet.

## Why do cats sleep so much?

Cats sleep when they're tired but also when they're bored.

It's normal for adult cats to be deeply asleep for only about 3 ½ hours a day. But they take lots of naps for a total of another 12 hours every day!

If your cat sleeps more than this, she might be sick. Or she might just need more toys and more playtime and attention from you.

## What plants, plant foods or people food are poisons for cats?

There are many plants that are bad for cats. Eating these plants can make them very ill, or even kill them.

Some of these plants are houseplants. Or they might grow in your garden. They are:

- Poinsettias (say this word like this: Poy-n-set-taz). Poinsettias are the plants with big red leaves that we often see around Christmas-time. Though they are beautiful, poinsettias are deadly for pets.

- Aloe. The sap in this plant's leaves sooth skin rashes and burns, including sunburn. But it is also poison for pets.

- Chrysanthemums, the garden flowers that are also called, "mums."

- Lilies

- Tulips

- Rhododendrons (say this word like this: ROW-doh-den-drons)

- Marijuana (say this word like this: Mare-i-wan-a)

- Mistletoe (say this word like this: MISS-ill-toe)

- Onions and all the plants in the onion family such as chives, garlic and leeks.

- Grapes and raisins.

Other people food that is poisonous for cats:

- Chocolate or any other food that has caffeine in it, such as tea, coffee, or soda pop.

- Chewing gum or candy with Xylitol in it. (Say this word like this: Zigh-let-tall). Xylitol is a chemical in sugarless gum, many types of candy and also in toothpaste.

- Wine, beer or anything with alcohol in it.

- Cookies or bread that are made with yeast.

Here are some other things you might have in your home or your garage, yard or garden that are dangerous for cats to eat:

- **Medicines meant for people**, especially aspirin or acetaminophen. Never give people medicine to pets unless your veterinarian recommends it. If your pet does accidently swallow any medicine, especially pills for coughs and colds, diet pills, or any pain pills, take your pet to the vet right away!

- **Vitamins and supplements** meant for people can harm your pets.

- **Dog food** (canned or dry food) and **canned tuna** meant for people does not have the nutrition cats need.

- **Tap water** has added chemicals and bleach in it. This is healthy for people, but not for cats. Give pets spring water or bottled water. Or pour out their drinking water and let it stand in an uncovered dish overnight (where your pets can't get it). The chemicals and bleach will mostly evaporate into the air, leaving the water safe to give to your pets.

- **Antifreeze** is good in cars, but deadly for pets.

- **Bleach** is useful for cleaning but also deadly for pets. **Moth balls** (used to prevent moths from chewing holes in towels, sheets and blankets) look like a toy ball to a cat, but they are also a dangerous poison for them.

- **Other poisons used in the garden** – weed-killer, rodent killer, mosquito and bug repellant – all are dangerous for pets.

Just like human children, pets need to be protected from harm.

## Why do cats like catnip?

As a plant, you would think that catnip would be something cats hate. But most cats love it! It makes

*This little kitten is playing with a toy that has catnip inside it.*

them feel happy and a little dizzy, something like smoking marijuana does for people.

Oddly, not all cats like catnip. But those who do show how much they like it by sniffing it, then licking or biting it. They often rub up against it, or try to roll in it while purring, meowing and even leaping up in the air for joy.

## Can cats see in colour?

Cats can see red, green and blue, but these colours probably aren't as bright for a cat as they are for humans.

Unlike humans, cats and dogs can see ultraviolet light. This might be to help feral and wild cats see the small animals they catch and eat. Cats can also see well when there is almost no light, something humans can't do.

## Can cats hear better than people?

Yes. Cats can also hear better than dogs.

Cats are able to hear sounds that are much higher than the top of the hearing range for people.

## How well can cats smell or taste things?

A cat's sense of smell is 14 times better than a person's sense of smell.

Cats smell with their noses, but also with a special scent organ that is at the top of their mouths. Called the Jacobson's organ, it helps a cat recognize smells.

## Besides purring, what other sounds can cats make?

Cats can make more than 100 different sounds, far more than dogs can. Cats can meow, hiss, purr or roar, yowl – and there are some odd cat sounds we have no words to describe!

## How to understand 'cat talk'

When cats meow very loudly, they want attention.

When their meow isn't loud, they want food.

A cat that walks around with his tail straight up in the air is happy.

A cat that wags her tail, or yawns, is annoyed.

Cats hiss to say, "Get away from me!" or "Leave me alone!"

When hissing doesn't work, they growl. A growl means, "Watch out or I will fight with you!"

A cat that hunches his back, with all his fur standing up, is angry.

If their fur is standing up just along their backbone and tail, they are about to attack!

A cat that crouches and flattens her ears, with her tail tucked very close to her body is frightened.

When cats are frightened or ill, they hide.

## Do cats understand people?

Do cats understand people talk? It seems they are able to learn many words, including their own names.

They probably can't 'read' the expressions on people's faces, but they can understand people. They use their excellent sense of smell to sense when people are stressed, upset, unhappy or sick.

Cats' faces don't have a lot of muscles. They can't smile, frown or laugh. Cats communicate with their bodies...and their eyes.

## Why do cats rub up against your leg or arm?

Cats have scent glands on their heads, faces and paw pads. They rub up against people they like to spread this scent. What this means to a cat is that you are her person. No other cat can have you!

*This little ginger tabby kitten is about four months old.*

## Why do cats have whiskers?

Cats use their whiskers to judge distance and space. So if a doorway isn't wide enough for them to walk through, their whiskers tell them. Cats can sense other things, such as a change in the air, with their whiskers. Cats that are blind can still walk around because their whiskers help them know where they are.

A cat's head whiskers are connected to their brain. The whiskers on the backs of their legs help them climb.

You should never cut your cat's whiskers. A cat that has his whiskers cut will be confused and scared. He will have trouble walking and jumping. A cat needs whiskers to survive!

## Why do cats bite?

If you are playing with your cat and suddenly she bites you, it means she really doesn't like what you're doing and you should stop it right now!

Cats bite when they feel threatened.

## Can people get sick from their cats?

Cats can get some of the same illnesses that people do, including colds, fever and more serious illnesses.

People do sometimes get sick because of cats, but this won't happen if you wash your hands before and after you touch your cat. If you get a cat scratch, always wash it right away with warm water and put on antiseptic. Keep it clean until it heals.

If your cat has watery eyes, a stuffy nose or is sneezing, they have a cold and need to see the vet.

## Can I teach my cat tricks?

Cats can't learn dog tricks like Play Dead or Roll Over.

Cats can be trained to come when you call them, sit nicely on your lap and use their litter box.

When a cat does something good, praise him. When he does something bad, hiss at him. Cats quickly learn what you expect them to do.

## Can dogs and cats be friends?

Yes they can.

Cats and dogs can learn to get along well together. Cats can also learn to be friends with other pets, such as bearded dragons or guinea pigs.

There can be problems when you already have one pet, and then suddenly there is a new pet in your home. Your 'old' pet might be jealous. Or he or she might worry that there won't be enough food.

Pets have to meet each other and get to know each other gradually. Never leave pets alone together until you are sure they are friends.

*Both this cat and pet bearded dragon enjoy thinking about being outside.*

# **Chapter Four**

# **How And Where To Get Your Pet Kitten Or Cat**

*This tabby kitten is about 4 months old.*

With so many to choose from, how can you pick out the right kitten or cat for you and your family?

Always choose the pet that is curious, playful and friendly. They need to be clean, with bright eyes, a pink mouth and gums, a cool soft nose and clean ears. All these are signs of excellent health.

You need to decide: do you want a kitten or an adult cat? Remember that kittens are lots of fun, but they need more time and care. Adult cats don't mind being alone all day while you're at school or at work.

Kittens might need more visits to the vet.

Adult cats already show their true personality – whether they are shy or very friendly, whether they mostly want to be left alone or always want to be on your lap, whether they are talkers or mostly quiet and other differences.

Some cats make lots of sounds. Some like cat toys, while others just ignore them. Some cats are good mousers, but others wouldn't care if a mouse walked right in front of them.

Every cat, just like every person, has their own character and quirks.

When you get a kitten, getting to know who they are is part of the fun.

When you get an adult cat, they already have their adult personality. They may also have some bad behaviour and find it hard to change to please you. But the good news is, they can if you are gentle and patient.

It isn't fair to any pet to get it and then decide you don't really like it. When you adopt a pet, you are making a promise that you will always give this animal everything they need to be healthy and happy for their entire life.

Make sure you choose the kitten or cat that you can make this promise to. Keep your promise!

*This cat lives at an animal shelter, waiting for a new family to adopt him.*

## Where to find your new pet

Maybe you have a family member of friend who has a cat they want to find a good new home for. Or their cat just had babies, and they agree that you can have one of the kittens.

Or you could look at the free online ads for your area. Often, someone is looking for good homes for kittens.

*Another place to look is at pet rescue shelters. Some* will have all kinds of pets available. Others specialize in finding new homes for kittens and cats. A big advantage of adopting your new pet from a pet rescue

*This is a Siamese cat.*

shelter is you are getting a pet that is healthy. And you are saving their life.

He or she has had all their shots and been checked by a vet to be sure they are ready to find their new home. Pets from shelters also have a tattoo in their ear or a microchip. This helps them get home if they are ever lost.

Most cats that you find at rescue shelters are mixed breed, tabbies, Bengals and, occasionally, a pure-breed cat.

Reasons to choose a particular breed of cat are that you like the way they look, you like their personality, or there is something else special about them.

If you want a special breed of cat, then you might go to a cat breeder. They are in the business of raising and selling healthy kittens.

Some cat breeds are:

- **Singapura** – a very small cat.

- **Siamese** – Known for their cream and brown coats, they are cats that talk a lot! They have pointy ears and their owners say they are especially smart.

- **Persian** cats have flat faces, long fur and very small ears.

- **Ragdoll** – a large, long-haired cat. If you choose a long-haired cat, remember that you will need to brush them every day.

- **Turkish Van** – is a breed of cat that, unlike almost all other cats, loves to swim!

- **Manx** cats are born without a tail.

- **Blue-point Himalayan** – a breed of small cats. The smallest one on record is Tinker Toy, who weighed just 1 pound 6 ounces (616 gm) and was only 2 ¾ inches (7 cm) tall.

- **Munchkins** are another very small cat breed.

- **Egyptian** or **Sphynx** cat – a cat that is almost completely bald. People who are allergic to cat dander can often have no problems when they live with a sphynx cat.

- **Tuxedo** – a black and white cat that looks like he or she is wearing a formal tuxedo suit. Kind of goofy, they are also wonderful acrobats!

There are many more breeds of cats – some with flat faces, very small ears, or thin faces – all bred for the way they look. If you want to know about what different breeds there are, you can see them at cat shows.

This is also the place to talk to cat breeders, if you decide you want a pure-bred kitten. These shows happen a few times a year in major cities. You can find them advertised online.

## How to choose a kitten

Be sure the kitten or cat you adopt is healthy. This is always true when you adopt from a shelter that is a registered charity, such as the Humane Society or SPCA. When you are given your new pet, or find them online, the first thing you will need to do is take them to the vet for a full check-up and shots.

Also, unless you intend to breed your cat, you need him or her to be neutered. This means a small operation to make sure she never has kittens or he causes a female cat to have kittens.

Cats that are neutered (or spayed) usually are healthier and live longer than if they are allowed to have kittens. There isn't a lot of difference between

*This black and white cat is known as a Tuxedo cat, or Felix cat.*

*This is a hairless Sphynx cat.*

female cats and males, after they are neutered. The operation means they might be a bit uncomfortable for a few days, but they soon forget about it.

There are already far more cats and kittens in the world than there are good homes to care for them. Responsible pet owners make sure to have their pets neutered. They don't let their pets add to the problem of far too many homeless cats.

If you choose to get your kitten or cat from a breeder, make sure he or she has been hand-raised in a good home that is clean. The kitten or cat you choose should be active and friendly.

Remember that a kitten allowed to stay with his or her mother and litter-mates for longer is more socialized. This means more able to be a good pet.

Don't choose an animal that has runny eyes, a runny nose, a cough or a dull coat. Don't take a pet home just because you feel sorry for him or her. If you do, they might need several visits to the vet. This could be expensive and they still might not survive. Choose a pet that is healthy and happy – they make the best pets.

If you live in United States, consider adopting a black cat. Because many Americans believe black pets are unlucky, often black dogs and cats are the last ones to find a home. This is unfair, because black pets can be just as wonderful (and lucky!) as any other colour.

Our family adopted Boots 16 years ago. He was found in winter in a cold, abandoned house. His family simply moved away and left him there alone. He was a pet and didn't know how to be a wild cat. If the Animal Rescue officers hadn't found him, he would have died.

You might also consider adopting a senior cat. While lots of people want kittens and very young cats, it is harder for deserving middle-aged or older cats to find a loving home.

## Where shouldn't you get your cat?

Kittens and cats in pet stores look just as cute as every other kitten or cat. But sometimes, this isn't the best place to find a healthy pet.

The reason is often pet stores get their animals from unethical breeders. Unethical means people who don't hand-raise the pets, so they aren't socialized (used to people).

*Boots waking from a cat nap.*

Unethical breeders don't bother about keeping animals in a clean, warm place or giving them enough heathy food. These kittens or cats might not have been wormed or had their shots. Unethical breeders don't care about animals. They just care about making money.

There are laws against abusing animals in many states, provinces and countries. Unfortunately, unethical breeders or other people who abuse animals don't always get caught. Do not help them continue to abuse animals by buying your pet from them.

By now, you probably have a good idea of what sort of cat you are going to get. But wait! Before you go ahead and adopt a pet, you need to get their new home ready to welcome them. Just like any new member to your family, they want to be comfortable and well cared for, so they can quickly feel right at home!

# I Want A Kitten Or A Cat

# <u>Chapter Five</u>

# Getting Ready For Your New Pet

If you have younger brothers or sisters, you already know that parents must make their homes safe for children. Some of the ways they do this is to put cleaning products away where children can't reach them, put covers on electrical outlets (power points) and pack away things that could break easily and hurt a baby or child, like glass ornaments.

They also need to get rid of anything with small pieces that a baby could put in her mouth. Sometimes, toys that are completely safe for older kids are very dangerous to babies and toddlers. If you have younger brothers and sisters, you probably already know there are some of your things you can't let them play with.

Good pet parents also have to make changes so their homes are safe for their pets.

What do you need to do to make your home kitten-safe, or safe for your new pet cat?

## Do this to kitten-proof, or cat-proof, your home

Kittens and cats run and jump a lot. They can easily knock things over, like empty glasses or lamps. Be sure that there are no heavy things that could fall on top of them and hurt them. Or fall on the floor and break.

All medicines need to be put away. Cats are curious and if something looks interesting or smells interesting, they could try to bite it. Or eat it.

In Jacquelyn's home, there are locks on all the lower cabinet doors in the kitchen. These are the same kind of locks that people buy to keep little children out of the cabinets. The reason is that their cat, Boots, likes to get in those cabinets and explore. But that's also where the cleaning supplies and kitchen garbage can are, so it's just not safe for him!

You also need to be sure that the screens on your windows are secure. You don't want your indoor cat slipping out the window and getting into trouble...or hit by a car.

Make sure there are no string, ribbon, rubber bands or bread bag plastic tabs left out. Cats could try to swallow these and choke.

Don't leave plastic bags from the grocery store out, either. Cats just love the crunchy sound plastic bags make – you could stuff a few into a plastic freezer bag, zip it closed and let them play with that.

Jacquelyn tells this story. "Don't make the same mistake our family did when we got their first cats. We thought they could use an old sock rolled up as a toy. Our cats thought this was great, but soon decided that all the socks in our house were toys!

"Not only this, they started 'stealing' and hiding our socks all over the house. There were socks behind the

*All cats scratch to keep their claws sharp. To stop them scratching your furniture, get them a scratching post like this one.*

sofa, under chairs, left on the stairs – everywhere. Once, a guest sat down on a chair, felt something lumpy, and pulled out a sock! Now we think it's pretty funny. But that day, it was very embarrassing."

Be careful that there are no lamp or computer chords, or chords from window blinds or curtains that your cat could get tangled in.

Keep the lid to your laundry machines closed. Kittens and cats love hiding places – including inside the washer or dryer.

Keep a tight lid on your recycling, compost and garbage cans that are in the house.

Houseplants need to be out of reach. Many are poisonous to kittens or cats.

Remember to always close the lid of the toilet. Cats sometimes think toilets are just fancy water bowls. They could fall in and drown.

If your home has a fireplace, keep the fire screen closed.

It's easy for a kitten or cat to get closed into a closet (fitted wardrobe) or dresser drawer. Always check before you close them.

Cats and kittens are able to get into some very small spaces. You might think they wouldn't want to, but cats do try to get behind the stove (hob) or other large pieces of furniture. Block those spaces so they can't get back there and possibly be hurt.

Some cats think it is tremendous fun to unwind all the toilet paper onto the floor. This isn't dangerous, just annoying! To stop them doing this, you need to buy toilet paper roll covers.

If your family likes to decorate your home for holidays, be sure that the decorations are out of reach for your pets. Cats think Christmas tree ornaments are more toys. But the glass balls can easily break into dangerously sharp pieces.

## When is a good time to adopt a new pet?

Some people think it is a good idea to give their family a new pet at Christmas time or other big holidays.

But here is something to think about. During the holidays, there's usually lots of rushing around. Friends come to visit. There are parties, lots more going on, and lots of excitement in the air. Pets can be stressed by all of these things.

To adjust happily to a new home, a pet needs calm, quiet, and a routine. He or she needs to have a chance to get comfortable and used to the new house rules. But during holidays, with all the strange smells of holiday foods, different people coming and going, and other activities of the season, pets can be very stressed. All these strange smells and sounds can overwhelm them.

At first, when they come into your home, a new pet kitten or cat needs to be in just one room, along with their food dish, water dish, litter box and some toys. They also need a few soft, warm places to sit. They feel comforted by a warm, secure place that is quiet.

Visit them several times during the day. Let them get used to you.

*To take your pet to the vet or for travel, you need a pet crate like this one. It should be big enough that your cat can stand up and turn around inside it.*

After a week or so, leave the door open, just a little bit. They will come out and start to explore when they are ready.

If you already have other pets, introduce them gradually.

Cats are territorial. This means they think they own the area they live in. They will fight other cats or dogs if they feel threatened.

When cats are wild, they live in colonies. However, they prefer to hunt and eat alone. Pet cats can happily get along with other pets, though they still prefer to be alone when they eat.

A kitten or cat that you adopt will think that it is scary to leave the home they know, and possibly also their mother, brothers and sisters, to come to your house. At first, you and your home will smell strange to them (and remember, cats have a MUCH better sense of smell that people do).

A new pet may cry at first. This is just them being homesick. They will soon get used to their new home if you are kind, gentle and patient with them.

## What is the best time to get a new pet?

Not a time when there is a lot going on in your home, such as during the Christmas or Easter or other major holidays.

Not a time when they will be alone for most of the day (though cats are better at being home alone than dogs are).

 Not right after a pet you had has died. This is a sad time. It isn't fair to a new animal to treat it like just a replacement for the friend you have lost. Give yourself some time to mourn and, eventually, be ready to welcome a new pet.

So when is a good time to get a pet? The answer is when you have the time to give him or her lots of care and attention. A time when you will not be rushing around, or stressed for some other reason, because animals are very good at 'reading' people's emotions and feelings.

A nervous home makes nervous pets. A quiet, calm home makes happier, better-behaved and healthier pets. And people.

We think the best time for kids to get pets is during summer vacation (school breaks). It's usually a time when people are happy and relaxed, when there is time to play and get to know each other, as friends do.

## What do you need to buy for your kitten, or cat?

1. A pet bed. Cats love sleeping anywhere that is warm and soft and feels safe. Just be sure that the pet bed you choose is easy for them to get into and out of.
2. Pet food and water bowls. These don't need to be fancy, but they should be sturdy and able to go in the dishwasher or easy to clean.
3. Kittens need kitten food, because they are still growing. Buy a good quality cat food if they are older than 8 months.
4. Indoor cats need a litter box. This is usually plastic, and looks like a big pan. It needs to have low sides that are easy for the kitten or cat to climb over.
5. Fill the litter box about ¾ full with a scoopable, unscented litter. Place their litter box in a quiet spot, far away from their food dish. If you have more than one cat, each one needs his or her own litter box. (If they have to share, there will be trouble!)
6. You will need a litter scoop to remove the poop from the litter box. An old slotted spoon works great. Or you can by a litter scoop online or at the pet store.
7. A sisal-covered scratching post. Cats need to scratch to keep their claws in good condition.

You can stop them scratching your furniture when you give them a scratching post.

8. A climbing cat tower. Cats love to look down on their territory (like your living room or sitting room).

9. A soft grooming brush.

10. Cat nail trimmers.

11. Toys. Cats love anything that looks like or moves like a mouse or a bird. They also like laser lights and will jump to try to 'catch' them. Just be careful to never point the light in their eyes. Another favourite toy for most cats is a stick with feathers at the end. You wave it around like a fishing pole and cats will leap and try to pounce on the feathers.

12. A cat crate. You need this for trips to the vet.

13. Cat treats. There are lots of different flavours – beef, chicken, tuna, salmon are some you'll see at the grocery store or pet shop.

Cats need toys to keep from being bored. They need a climbing tower to get some exercise. And they need treats for the same reason you do!

They love hiding places, especially empty boxes or suitcases. They love looking out the window.

They usually are happy in a family, but become especially attached to one person in their family. Usually, it's the person who spends the most time with them and fills their food dish.

They are very fussy about staying clean. Cats spend a third of their time washing and grooming themselves. When cats live together, they will groom each other.

And if you don't clean the litter box often enough, they will let you know they aren't pleased!

Just like all little children and most people, cats like routines. They like to know that their food dish will never be empty, there will always be fresh water to drink and warm places to snooze.

Cats are snackers. They eat a few mouthfuls of food several times a day.

Lots of people think they should get a cat because, they say, "cats are easy. They don't really need anything."

This isn't true. Cats don't need much...but they do need what all people need. Fresh air to breathe, clean water, healthy food, warmth, shelter and protection from harm and a good home.

When they are sick, they need medical care from a vet and they may need cat medicine.

The thing they need most is your loving kindness and friendship.

*Cats love to play in cardboard boxes.*

# I Want A Kitten Or A Cat

# Chapter Six

# Good Care For Kittens And Cats

Cats sometimes seem to be able to get along pretty well without people. But they can't be happy as pets without good care from their owners.

One of the first things you need to know about kittens and cats is how to pick them up. Do this wrong and they could be hurt. Or they could scratch and hurt you. They wouldn't mean to do this. It is just their instinct to protect themselves.

Here's how to safely pick up a kitten or a cat

First, put one hand under the cat. Be sure all his weight is on your hand.

Put your other hand on top of the kitten or cat, to steady them and so they won't try to leap away.

If you have a big or heavy cat, like a Maine Coon or Ragdoll cat, it might be better not to try to carry him or her around. Sit on the floor to play with them or pet them. Or let them sit on your lap.

Their mother lifts them up by the scruff of their neck when they are tiny kittens. This is not how you can lift a larger kitten or cat.

## Things to never do with your cat

Never do this:

- Pick them up by their tail, the skin behind their neck, or their paw or leg

- Give them dog food, dinner leftovers or bones to chew

- Let them chew on electrical cords

- Hit them

- Yell at them

- Squirt water at them. They don't understand this. All they learn is to be afraid of you.

## Ears, Teeth, Claws and Fur

Does your mother remind you to wash your hands and face, and don't forget your neck and ears?

Does your father tell you to remember to brush your teeth?

It turns out that you need to remember these things for your pet cat, too!

Cats need their teeth cleaned to prevent tooth decay. Do this with a toothbrush and special pet toothpaste. Don't use toothpaste meant for people. It has a chemical in it called Xilitol that is poison for cats. You could also use a clean, soft cloth that is dampened in warm water to gently clean your cat's teeth.

Cats don't like this. You may need help holding them firmly and holding their mouth open. Unfortunately, you can't tell them this is so they won't have teeth that hurt. Try to be as gentle and fast at the tooth cleaning as possible.

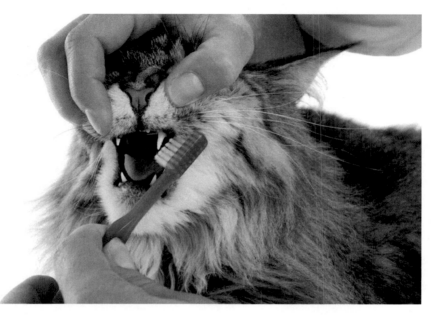

*Cats are not fond of having their teeth brushed. But, like this Maine Coon cat, they need their teeth cleaned to avoid painful tooth decay.*

You also need to clean their ears. The soft cloth that is just a bit wet with warm water works for this. Never use a cotton-tip stick.

A cotton ball or soft face cloth dipped in warm water is good for cleaning their ears, nose, around their eyes, their face and under their chin. These are all the places a cat has difficulty washing themselves.

Generally, it isn't a good idea to give a cat a bath. It can leave them with itchy skin. But if you must bathe your cat, use cat shampoo. People shampoo is not good for their coat. And never spray them with room freshener or a cleaning product. They could try to lick it off and be poisoned!

*Long-haired cats like this Persian kitten need to be brushed every day.*

All cats need to be brushed. For long-hair cats, this is at least every day. Short-hair cats only need to be brushed twice a week.

Brush gently, starting with their head and working towards their tail. You need a wire brush for long-hair cats and a bristle brush for short-hair cats. Some cats really enjoy being brushed, but others just don't like it. If your cat objects to the brushing, just do it for a minute or so, then finish the job later.

Cats need their claws trimmed, just like you need your fingernails and toenails trimmed from time to time. For cats, you nip off just the very sharp tip of the claws. If you cut their claws too short, it will be painful for your cat. It's just like if someone cut your fingernails too short. They would hurt until they grew longer.

Some cat owners think it's a good idea to have a cat's claws removed because a cat that has no claws can't claw the furniture or the curtains. But think how you'd feel if someone yanked out all your fingernails. It would be intensely painful. Cats feel pain just as much as people do.

Having their claws removed is even worse than if your fingernails were removed. The reason is that when cats are declawed, they also lose a piece of the bone the claw grows out of. It would be like you having the ends of your fingers cut off.

And remember, cats walk on their claws. If they are declawed, it is several weeks before they're able to walk again.

For these reasons, it's cruel to cut away a cat's claws.

## Signs you need to go to the vet

When kittens have their teeth, face, eyes and ears cleaned the way we have just told you about, they get used to it. They may not like it, but they put up with it because they know you will be gentle.

If you adopt your cat when she or he is older, they may be what is called "paw shy." This means they don't really like people touching their paws, mouth, ears or anywhere on their face.

If so, here's what to do: gently stroke their head for a short time and then give them one cat treat.

Do this for a week or so, and they will know you won't hurt them when you touch their head. Plus, they will get a treat.

Gradually, they will let you clean their eyes, ears, teeth, face and chin. Of course, they will still expect to get the treat when you do this. But that's okay – just wipe their teeth one last time after they crunch the treat.

If you cuddle them a bit, then gently clip just one paw's claw tips, then do some more cuddling, they will learn that this is OK, too.

## How to take your cat to the vet

If you keep your cat crate out, with the door open, and a towel or cushion inside to make it more comfortable, your kitten will decide that being in her crate isn't a scary thing.

And if you sometimes close the crate and take her for a short car ride, she will decide that car rides aren't so bad, either.

Before Jacquelyn's family knew this, they made a bad mistake with their cat, Baby. Baby was a cat that didn't like car rides and was especially afraid of going to the vet.

She hated vets and would try to attack them! It was very stressful for everyone when Baby wasn't well and needed help from the vet.

You can teach your cat to behave at the vet's. It is much better to 'drop in' for a visit or two to your vet's office, just to say "hello" and let your pet know that it might be strange (and smell strange) to go to the vet,

*Cats need their nails clipped just like people do. Ask your vet to show you how to do it so you don't cut your cat's nails too short and cause them pain.*

but it isn't a reason to try to bite the people who are trying to help you.

It's also a good idea to take your cat to the vet for an annual check-up.

When does your cat need to see the vet?

## These are reasons to see your vet:

When you first get your pet, take them to meet the vet and have a general examination to be sure they are healthy and have had all their shots.

If your cat has a stuffy nose, is sneezing, has watery eyes or is coughing, they may have a cold or something more serious. Until you can get to the vet, you can use a baby aspirator to gently remove the mucous from their nose. You can find baby aspirators at the grocery store or drug store (pharmacy).

When your cat has a bad odour (he's smelly) see the vet. It could be because of tooth decay. Vets are also pet dentists.

Most cats sleep a lot. But if your cat is sleeping all the time, and seems to have no energy, she could be sick. This is also true if your cat's personality changes suddenly.

Cats are very good at hiding how they really feel, especially when they are in pain. A cat that is purring loudly, trembling or shivering, or hiding all the time is in pain.

Get to the vet immediately if your cat swallows something that is poison for them, like chocolate, mistletoe or poinsettias.

A cat that stops using their litter box, suddenly loses weight, won't eat, has diarrhea (diarrhoea) or constipation, is constantly vomiting, is bleeding and it won't stop, has breathing problems or has been hit by a car needs the vet immediately.

Keep your vet's number near the phone or where you can get it quickly. Call them and ask what to do. They will probably tell you to come to their office.

## How to give a pill to a cat

Sometimes, the vet will send you home with medicine to give your cat. Your vet will show you how to do this, but here's a reminder:

1. Gently open your cat's mouth (but not too wide).

2. Flip the pill to the back of her mouth.

3. Gently hold her jaws closed while holding her head as if she was looking up at the ceiling.

4. Gently stroke her neck until she swallows.

5. Check her mouth to make sure the pill went down.

## Senior cats

If you adopt (or you have) a senior cat, you might have noticed that their behaviour changes when they get older.

Many senior cats become more talky, and they also get louder. This might be because their own hearing isn't as good as it was, or because they are ill.

They might sleep more. And snore.

They might change in what they like to eat.

They might also have trouble keeping their food down, meaning that you have to clean up after them. This can be annoying, but remember that sometimes when you get sick you also get more noisy with coughing, or complain, or might throw up. It isn't the cat being a 'bad' cat, it's just they don't feel completely like themselves.

## How to help an overweight cat

Just like people, cats can have weight problems. This might be because they ate too much unhealthy food, didn't get enough exercise, or have an illness that causes obesity. (Obesity is the term doctors and vets use when a person or a pet is very overweight).

The fattest cat ever known was Himmy, a tabby who lived in Australia. He weighed 47 pounds (21.3 kg). That is way too much, even for the bigger breeds of pet cats like Maine Coon and Ragdoll, which are healthy at about half that weight.

For most cat breeds, a healthy weight is about 10 pounds (4.5 kg).

Here's how you can help your overweight kitty slim down. You need to do this, because overweight cats suffer discomfort, pain and don't live as long as cats that are a healthy weight for their breed. They may get so big they can't get into their litter box anymore. This is unpleasant for everyone.

Don't ever give your cat people food or dog food. They can't have bread, cookies, gravy or dripping from the pan after meat is cooked, ice cream, candies (sweets), gum or canned meats meant for humans. The only thing that is really healthy for cats to eat is cat food.

Switch your overweight cat to wet food (soft cat food). It's higher in protein and has less carbs than dry food. Cut out all cat treats.

You should take your cat to the vet and ask for his advice before putting your pet on a weight-loss diet. It might be that your cat has an illness that is causing the weight gain.

# Seven

# No More Bad Cats!

Have you seen those videos online with bad cats causing all sorts of mischief? There is the one where the cat jumps on the piano keys when her owner is practicing. Or the cat that looks straight at his owner, then pushes a glass to the very edge of the table with his paw and waits to see what will happen next.

And the video with the cat that's told not to scratch the chair leg, but goes right on doing it.

To people, it might seem that cats are being 'bad' on purpose, just to annoy us.

But to cats, they're just doing what comes naturally to them. Jumping up to be near their owners, playing with objects and scratching to sharpen their claws are all behaviours that cats learned over millions of years. If you're a cat, that's what you do.

And this 'bad' behaviour doesn't stop there.

Boots walks around the house yodelling loudly, after everyone else has gone to bed. There doesn't seem to be any reason, he just does it.

He also does a lot of kneading on our laps before he sits down to purr. The sitting and purring are nice; the kneading not so much. Tiny kittens are born knowing how knead, which is pressing back and forth with their paws. They do this to their mother's belly to get more milk.

*Our pet cat Baby loved to hide inside a cozy blanket.*

Cats never forget this kneading behaviour. They do it even as adults and even when they become senior cats. It seems to give them comfort.

Some cats are very talky. You might wish they would just be quiet, for once.

Some are always jumping up on the counter (worktop) searching for food they shouldn't have, even when there is healthy cat food in their dish.

Some will get into the kitchen garbage, spreading it all over the floor, if you don't put a tight lid on the garbage container that they can't open.

Some, like Baby in Jacquelyn's family, like to steal socks from the laundry basket and hide them everywhere.

And some cats seem to like to pester people who visit your home and would rather not have a cat on their lap.

Do cats do all these things on purpose? Yes, they do, because to your cat, doing all these things makes purr-fect sense.

But not to their owners. So what can you do?

## What to do about 'bad' cat behaviour

While cats refuse to learn how to do tricks, you can train your cat to have better manners.

Cats use yowling, growling and hissing to communicate with each other, or with another animal. They use meowing and purring only when they want to talk to people.

There are lots of reasons for cats to talk too much or too loudly. Some are good reasons – like telling you her water dish is empty, she can't reach her litter box or it needs to be cleaned, or she's trapped in a room. When your cat is noisy, you always need to check and figure out why.

- She wants food. If your cat meows loudly every time someone walks out to the kitchen, get an automatic feeder that opens at set times (4 or 5 times a day). She'll soon learn when food is available and stop begging.

- He wants attention. This means your pet needs more time with you, playing, being brushed or just talking to him.

- They might be stressed. Just like people, cats worry when there's a big change in their home. A new baby, moving, a family member being sick or leaving home, or making major changes to your home like putting in a new kitchen or bathroom are all stressful for the people and for the pets. Your upset cat will be soothed by extra attention and quiet time.

- Cats that are ill or getting old talk more. If a cat is hungry, thirsty or in pain, it will usually do more meowing. Senior cats often develop kidney disease or thyroid disease. Both illnesses cause them to be more noisy.

- Female cats that can still have babies and want to (this is called being in heat) make a lot more noise, and so do the males who want to be with them. The answer is to have your pet neutered. This will also prevent unwanted kittens.

## How can I stop my cats from fighting?

All kittens enjoy play-fighting and chasing each other. Playing is fun for them. It's also how they learn the skills adult cats need.

Cat fighting is different. When cats are playing, there might be some hissing, but there is usually no loud howling or wailing. No one gets hurt.

When two cats avoid each other for a while afterwards, it was a fight.

If they still want to groom each other and sleep next to each other, it was just playing.

When you adopt two kittens, they usually grow up as friends. But if you already have an adult cat and adopt a kitten, they might have trouble getting along.

If you have two cats that are always fighting, you will need to separate them. Then, gradually, re-introduce them to each other. Give both lots of attention so there will be no jealousy.

## How can you make a cat stop scratching furniture?

Cats scratch to stretch their muscles, sharpen their claws and mark their territory.

From the time they are kittens, cats need to learn what they are allowed to scratch. To teach them, you will need to cover places they are not allowed to scratch with plastic, double-sided tape or aluminum foil. This doesn't look good, but it makes these places unattractive to your cat. When he learns where he can scratch, you can take the plastic, tape or foil off your furniture.

You could also spray your furniture with lemon or lime spray. This is a pleasant odour for people. Cats dislike citrus odours because they are allergic to citrus foods, so they will avoid anything that smells like citrus fruits. You need to remember to keep spraying the furniture with the lemon or lime spray every few days, until your cat loses interest in that piece of furniture.

Cats develop their favourite scratching places. If you get your cat a scratching post but he just ignores it, try putting catnip on the scratching post. That way your cat will know it's his.

You could use regular catnip that you rub in, or you can get catnip spray online or at pet stores.

Here's what doesn't work: grabbing your cat's paws and showing him how to scratch his scratching post. This just feels weird to a cat. They don't understand.

## What can you do about pet stains?

Pets that are very stressed, sick or very old might leave pet stains on your bed, furniture, cushions, rugs or their bed.

If normal washing with soap and warm water doesn't get rid of the stains, or on chairs, use pet stain remover. Buy it online or at pet stores. It works when you follow the instructions on the bottle.

## How should you discipline your kitten or cat?

Losing your temper with your cat doesn't work. Shouting at her, or hitting, shaking or slapping will just make them not like you. It won't change their behaviour. Also, doing any of these things is cruel.

The name for being cruel to animals is "animal abuse."

It is much better to talk to a cat that is doing something wrong in a firm voice. Or hiss at them. Cats understand hissing.

You must catch them right when they are doing the 'bad' behaviour. Wait even a few seconds afterwards and the cat won't know what you're hissing about.

It's also important to be consistent (say this word like this: con-sis-tent). Consistent means having a routine and always doing things the same way.

You can't play roughly with your kitten or cat one day, then be angry the next day when your cat wants to play rough some more. Cats, like people, like to know what to expect. It makes them a little bit crazy when the rules are always changing. This is true for people, too.

## Should you get two cats so they have a companion?

Like young children, kittens get scared when they are home alone. It doesn't help them if you leave music playing or a radio turned on when you are away from home. Music doesn't have any meaning for cats. It's just odd sounds. They'd much rather hear natural sounds, like birds singing and calling to each other.

It's a good idea to have two cats to keep each other company. Ideal is to adopt two kittens at the same time. They will quickly learn to be friends and will be happier and less anxious when everyone is away at school or at work.

And it's a lot of fun to watch kittens playing together!

*Cats that live together will groom each other. This means they help keep each other clean.*

# Chapter Eight

# What To Name Your New Pet Kitten

If you adopt a kitten, he or she probably won't already have a name. An adult cat probably might already have a name, but adult cats can learn to answer to a new name if you really don't like their 'old' name.

Cats seem to like having names that end in "ie" or "y." Maybe this is just a sound they like, or it could just be easier for them to hear, when most of the sounds people make are words they can't understand.

Here are some "ie" cat names:

**For a female cat:**

- Lacey
- Kellie
- Suzie
- Bettie
- Laurie
- Lucie
- Jenny
- Zoey
- Lily

- Missy
- Daisy
- Poppy
- Millie

**For a male cat:**

- Bertie
- Billy
- Jimmie
- Toby
- Tony
- Petey
- Freddie
- Stevie
- Bobby
- Charlie
- Teddy
- Curlie
- Timmie
- Tommy
- Smokey

Or you could pick a cute cat name, like Boots, Tiger, Tiny, Socks, Peanut, Puss, Smudge, Twinkle or Princess.

Or how about a fluffy name, like Baby, Coco, Tiger, Tigger, Puff, Puss, Darling, Sweetie, Silky, Lovie or Cutie?

And here are some more ideas: Angel, Devil, Spirit, Ghost, Goblin and Scout.

In this book you've learned everything you need to know to become a proud new pet parent to a kitten or a cat.

You've learned a bit about how a cat thinks, what they like and what they want and need to be healthy and happy.

We've told you how to choose your new pet, where to find him or her and how to help them become a wonderful new addition to your family.

# **Thank You!**

*This white cat is best friends with a pet bearded dragon.*

Thanks so much for reading this book. We really hope you enjoyed it! If you did, could you help other kids and their parents and teachers find out about this book series? You can do it by writing a review on Amazon or in Goodreads. We'd really appreciate it!

And if you love reading about pets, we'll be happy to let you know when we publish our next pet book. Just send an email to: Jacquelyn@CrimsonHillBooks.com

Best wishes,

**Tristan & Jacquelyn**

# About Tristan & Jacquelyn

Tristan Pulsifer is 9 years old and is in grade 4. His family has a houseful of pets! There are seven pets in their family: two dogs, a cat, three leopard geckos and a bearded dragon. The Pulsifer family dogs are called Sophie and Molly. Their cat is Max and the lizards are Rosie, Nico, Gizmo and Lewie.

Tristan lives next door to Jacquelyn Elnor Johnson, who is a book writer. Her family has just one pet right now, a senior cat named Boots. But she has happy memories of many dogs she has owned and known, including Poodles, Dachshunds, Collies and a Labrador Retriever.

Tristan and Jacquelyn like to get together to watch movies, eat treats, play card games and write books about pets.

They live in Nova Scotia, Canada.

# More Fun Books For Kids Who Love Pets!

Read more great pet books from Crimson Hill Books!

## Best Pets for Kids series:

I Want A Leopard Gecko

I Want A Bearded Dragon

I Want A Puppy Or A Dog

I Want A Kitten Or A Cat

## Fun Animal Facts for Kids series:

Fun Dog Facts For Kids 9-12

Fun Cat Facts For Kids 9-12

Fun Leopard Gecko and Bearded Dragon Facts For Kids 9-12

Fun Reptile Facts For Kids 9-12

## Fun Pets for Kids series:

Small Fun Pets: Beginning Pets For Kids 9-12

Top 10 Fun Pets for Kids 9-12

Investigate more books for curious kids right here:

# www.BestPetsForKids.fun

Made in the USA
Lexington, KY
14 December 2018

# Winter Holidays

by Lana Cruce

illustrated by Diana Kizlauskas

PEARSON

Scott
Foresman

Editorial Offices: Glenview, Illinois • Parsippany, New Jersey • New York, New York
Sales Offices: Needham, Massachusetts • Duluth, Georgia • Glenview, Illinois
Coppell, Texas • Ontario, California • Mesa, Arizona

Selene lives in Chicago, Illinois, with her parents and her two younger sisters, Gwen and Corinna.

The family lives in a brick townhouse with planters in every window that grow bright red geraniums in the summertime. They have a kitten named Suki and two fat, lazy goldfish.

Selene loves to play soccer and invent games of make-believe with her little sisters. Sometimes they are explorers, digging in the closets for dinosaur bones. Other times they are master chefs at a fancy restaurant or astronauts on a new planet.

One December, school was out for winter break. Even though it was too cold to play soccer, Selene didn't have any trouble staying busy. She drew pictures, read books, and played with her sisters and her friends.

Selene has a special friend named Anneka. Anneka is Selene's pen pal from Stockholm, Sweden.

Sometimes Selene and Anneka exchange letters by mail, along with pictures or short stories they write for each other. Other times they send e-mails, which are much faster. It takes about a week for a letter to reach Sweden in the mail from Illinois, but only a minute to send an e-mail message.

Like Selene, Anneka has two younger
siblings, and she loves to draw. She is also
eight years old. She lives with her parents,
her brother, Oskar, and her baby sister,
Astrid. Anneka's family lives in an old
farmhouse with a pond behind it. They keep
goats and chickens. Anneka likes to skate on
the pond in the winter.

Anneka looks forward to getting mail
from Selene, who is far away in a country
she has never visited. Selene's letters and
drawings always make Anneka laugh.
Selene's stories give her good ideas for
make-believe games to play with her
younger brother.

After lunch one day, Selene sent an e-mail to Anneka. She wrote about how Suki had tried to catch one of the goldfish and splashed water on the floor. She also wrote about the snowball fight she and her sisters had that morning. At the end of her e-mail, she added, "P.S. It's almost time for Kwanzaa!"

The next day, Selene eagerly read Anneka's reply. Anneka wrote about the book she had just finished reading and told a funny story about her baby sister. At the end of the email she wrote, "P.S. What is Kwanzaa?"

Selene found her father in the living room with Gwen and Corinna.

"Daddy, my friend Anneka doesn't know what Kwanzaa is," she said. "I want to tell her about it, but I'm not sure what to say. I know what we do on Kwanzaa, but I don't even know how it started."

"Kwanzaa started in the 1960s, when African Americans were fighting for their civil rights, which are freedoms that all people should have," Selene's father began. "An African American man named Maulana Karenga wanted to teach people about their history. Kwanzaa is a time to celebrate our African culture. It is a time for a special ceremony and for being with your family."

"What does the word *kwanzaa* mean?" asked Gwen, Selene's little sister.

Selene knew the answer. "*Kwanzaa* is a word from the Swahili language," she told Gwen. "It means 'the first fruits'. "

Their father smiled. "I think you know more about Kwanzaa than you think."

Selene wrote a letter to Anneka. She explained that Kwanzaa starts on December 26, and it lasts for seven days.

Selene told Anneka her family would gather to honor their ancestors and their culture. They would decorate a Kwanzaa bush with homemade ornaments. They would set a table with an ear of corn for each child in the family. They would also set out a carved cup, or *kikombe*, for the grown-ups.

"Every night," Selene wrote, "we will light the *kinara*, which is a seven-holed candleholder. The candles are black, red, and green, and each one represents a different value, such as responsibility, faith, and creativity.

"On the last night of Kwanzaa, we will exchange homemade gifts and have a big feast. I can't wait!"

Selene finished her letter. Then she drew pictures for Anneka of all the Kwanzaa symbols she had talked about.

A week later, Selene got a reply from Anneka. It read:

Dear Selene,

Thank you for telling me about Kwanzaa. I wish I could see your family celebrating this holiday. The last night sounds like fun! Now I want to tell you about the holiday we are going to be celebrating soon called Luciadagen. It means Saint Lucia Day.

The festival of Saint Lucia is celebrated on December 13, which is one of the longest, coldest, and darkest nights of the winter in Sweden.

The story of Saint Lucia is that during the Middle Ages, a horrible famine happened in Sweden. People didn't have food to eat. Saint Lucia appeared dressed in white wearing a crown of lights on her head. She brought food to the hungry villagers.

My family honors Saint Lucia by lighting candles, eating special foods, and singing carols.

Early in the morning, the oldest daughter of the family (that's me!) goes to her parents' bedroom, wearing a crown and a white dress with a red belt. The crown is made from sprigs of lingonberry. This plant symbolizes new life during the cold winter.

My mom used to wear a crown with real candles when she was little! The candles in my crown work with batteries. When I go to my parents' room, I take them a special breakfast of *lussekatts*, which are buns with raisins in them.

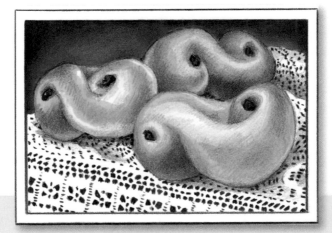

Younger daughters follow Lucia, as her angel helpers. Younger brothers follow dressed as star boys. They wear white robes and pointed hats and carry star-topped wands. This will be the first Saint Lucia Day for my little sister, Astrid. She's too young to walk behind me, so she is going to wear a white dress and Oskar is going to carry her.

After the morning celebration I'll go to school. My classmates and I will choose one girl to play Lucia. The girl will wear her candle crown and hand out lussekatts and gingerbread to everyone. She will also lead the class in a special song called "Santa Lucia." Last year, my friend Dagmar got to play Lucia. I hope this year it will be me! At the end of the day, we will all go outside to watch a candlelight parade down the streets of Stockholm.

Selene thought that the festival of Saint Lucia sounded like fun. She thanked Anneka for teaching her about the holiday.

"I wish I could see you and your family celebrating Luciadagen!" she wrote.

The night before Saint Lucia Day, Selene's mother helped her and her sisters make gingerbread.

"It's too bad we don't have the recipe for lussekatts," said Selene. "Gingerbread cookies will have to do."

Selene, Gwen, and Corinna all found white dresses that they could wear and some thick red ribbon to tie around Selene's waist. They made a crown from cardboard and sprigs of pine needles. Their father found some battery-operated lights to attach to it.

The next morning, Selene woke up early. She got her younger sisters out of bed and brought them down to the kitchen to prepare a tray of gingerbread and coffee. The girls put on their dresses, and Gwen and Corinna helped fasten the crown in Selene's hair.

The girls walked up the stairs into their parents' room, waking them with cries of "Happy Saint Lucia Day!" Their parents laughed and rubbed their eyes. They sat up and took their breakfast trays.

"I like this tradition!" Selene's mother said, taking a bite of the gingerbread.

A week later it was time for Kwanzaa. Selene and her sisters decorated the house and the Kwanzaa bush with flowers made of red, green, and black paper. Each night after dinner, the family gathered in the living room to light a candle on the kinara.

On the last night of Kwanzaa, Selene gave her mother a jewelry box she had made and decorated with brightly colored beads. She gave her father five bookmarks that she had painted. She gave Gwen a little book she had written, and Corinna a paper doll she had made. After dinner the party began.

At the end of the evening, Selene's grandfather gave the final speech, and then they all went to bed.

That same day in Sweden, Anneka was wrapping some gifts she had made for her family. She made a walking stick for her father with his initials carved into the wood. She made her mother a painting of her favorite hen. She made Oskar a drum, and for Astrid, a mobile with bright blue ribbon and bells that jingled.

"Happy Kwanzaa!" she exclaimed, giving each of her family members a package.

"What is this?" asked her father, laughing.

As her family opened their gifts, Anneka explained about Kwanzaa.

"I think this is a great tradition," said her mother, hugging her tightly.

A few weeks later, Selene got a letter in the mail from Anneka. Anneka wrote that she had been chosen to play Lucia at school. She also wrote about celebrating the final day of Kwanzaa with her family. She included a picture of her family on Saint Lucia Day and on Kwanzaa.

Selene thought about holidays and celebrations. Although Kwanzaa and Saint Lucia Day are different, they are both about being with your family and remembering your history. Selene was happy that she and Anneka had taught each other so much. She felt lucky to have a friend from another country.

Selene went to her room and wrote a reply to Anneka. She told her about the gifts she had made her family members for Kwanzaa and about all the different foods at the party. She also told Anneka how much fun she had playing Saint Lucia and making the crown with her sisters. In the envelope she included a photograph of herself wearing the crown of pine needles. She also drew a picture of her and her sisters bringing their parents gingerbread and coffee. As she was addressing the letter, Selene's sister Gwen stuck her head in the door.

"Ask your friend Anneka to teach us about more Swedish holidays," said Gwen.

# Cultural Celebrations

Almost all cultural groups have celebrations or festivals. Chinese New Year is celebrated in February with parades and fireworks. Families eat foods they hope will bring good luck: chicken for prosperity, a whole fish for togetherness, and long noodles for long life.

In Basel, Switzerland, people have celebrated *Fasnacht* since the Middle Ages. For this carnival, there is music and dancing, and people wear masks and fancy costumes.

People in Basel, Switzerland, celebrate Fasnacht.